Books in the Linkers series

Homes discovered through Art & Technology
Homes discovered through Geography
Homes discovered through History
Homes discovered through Science

Myself discovered through Art & Technology
Myself discovered through Geography
Myself discovered through History
Myself discovered through Science

Toys discovered through Art & Technology
Toys discovered through Geography
Toys discovered through History
Toys discovered through Science

Water discovered through Art & Technology
Water discovered through Geography
Water discovered through History
Water discovered through Science

Food discovered through Art & Technology
Food discovered through Geography
Food discovered through History
Food discovered through Science

Journeys discovered through Art & Technology
Journeys discovered through Geography
Journeys discovered through History
Journeys discovered through Science

First published 1997 A&C Black (Publishers) Limited
35 Bedford Row, London WC1R 4JH

ISBN 0-7136-4769-8
A CIP catalogue record for this book is available from the British Library.

Commissioned photographs by Zul Mukhida
Design by Jean Wheeler

Acknowledgements

Advertising Archives; 5 (left), 18 (left), Beamish; 2, 3 (both), 4, 5 (right), 6 (both), 7, 8, 9 (both), 10, 11 (left), 12 (both), 13, 14 (left), 15, 16, 17 (right), 18 (right), 20, 21 (both), 22 (left), James Davis; 23, Robert Opie; 14 (right), 17 (left), 19.

Every effort has been made to contact copyright holders of any material reproduced in this book. Any omissions will be rectified in future printings if notice is given to the Publisher.

Printed and bound in Italy by L.E.G.O.

Journeys

discovered through History

Karen Bryant-Mole

Contents

A & C Black • London

Journeys

When people make journeys, they travel from one place to another.
Over time, there have been many changes in the way journeys are made.

Horses

Before the invention of engines, most journeys on land were made in vehicles pulled by horses.
The photograph on the left was taken about a hundred years ago. It shows a horse-drawn tram.
Horses were also used to pull carts, carriages and buses.

Engines

The train in the photograph above was powered by a steam engine. The invention of the steam engine made the first important change to travel.
Later, came the internal combustion engine.
This is the type of engine that cars have.

Variety

The photograph below shows a typical street scene in 1905.
You can see lots of different kinds of vehicles.
Horse-drawn vehicles continued to be used for many years after the invention of engines.

This book will take a closer look at how and why journeys have been made during the past one hundred years.

Cars

The car replaced the horse and carriage.
An early nickname for the car was 'the horseless carriage'.

Expensive
The first cars were hand-built. Each car took a long time to make.
They were very expensive and only rich people could afford them.

The man in this 1900s photograph is a chauffeur. Many car owners employed a chauffeur to drive them around.

Cheaper

This is a 1919 photograph of a Model T Ford. Model T Fords took less time to make than earlier cars and were much cheaper to buy. Motoring was no longer only for rich people.

Families

By the 1950s, when this advert appeared, many more people owned a car. The advert showed how easy it was to fit the whole family into a small car. Today, lots of families own a car.

Cars have allowed people the freedom to go where they want, when they want. But they have also led to traffic jams and pollution.

Two wheels

Cycling clubs
A hundred years ago, cycling was very fashionable.
Many people belonged to cycling clubs.
The picture on the right shows members of a cycling club in 1902.

Countryside
Bicycles gave people a freedom they had never had before.
They could cycle out from the towns into the countryside.
The photograph on the left, taken in 1908, shows cyclists enjoying a picnic.

Motorbikes

Early motorbikes were really just bicycles with engines attached. The woman in this 1910s photograph is sitting in a sidecar, which is fixed on to the motorbike.
Sidecars were a popular way for women to travel.

Bikes and motorbikes are still used today. They are cheaper to run than cars and can get through traffic jams easily.

Public transport

Public transport is transport that can be used by everyone.

Buses

A hundred years ago, buses were usually pulled by horses. The people who travelled on the top of this bus sat in the open air. The route the bus took was written on the side, so people knew where it was going.

Trams

Trams were popular in towns.
Unlike buses, trams ran along rails.
The first trams were pulled by horses.
Later, they were powered by electricity.
The photograph on the right shows an electric tram from the 1900s.
Like buses, trams ran along a set route at set times.

Taxis

A taxi travels when and where you choose.
Early taxis were small horse-drawn carriages, called cabs.
The horses and cabs in the 1910s picture on the left are lined up, waiting for customers.

Today, we can still travel by bus and taxi, although the vehicles now look very different.
In cities, trams are becoming popular again, as they are cheap to run and don't pollute the air.

Trains

Passengers

This 1930s photograph shows a steam train. It travelled between London and Edinburgh, pulling passenger carriages.

Some trains had special passenger carriages called Pullmans. Pullmans were very comfortable, with armchairs for passengers to sit in.

Goods

The 1940s steam train on the right is carrying coal.
Trains that carry goods are called freight trains.
Today, many goods are transported by lorry and there are fewer freight trains.

Diesel

The photograph on the left was taken in 1968. By then, most trains were powered by diesel engines rather than steam engines.
Diesel engines were cleaner than steam engines. Unlike steam engines, they didn't need a coal fire or a supply of water.

Today, most long distance trains still have diesel engines but many local trains run on electricity.

Roads

A hundred years ago, many roads were muddy and full of holes. This made journeys slow and uncomfortable.

Stone

Roads were less likely to get damaged if they had a hard, waterproof surface.
Some roads were made from round stones, called cobbles, or stone blocks, called sets.
The 1890s photograph on the left shows a group of workmen laying sets.

Traffic

As the amount of traffic increased, more roads were needed.
The photograph below, taken in 1950, shows workers building a by-pass.
Instead of having to drive through the middle of town, by-passes allow people to go around the edge.

Chippings

The photograph above was taken in the 1910s. Stone chippings were shovelled out of the truck and on to the road. The steam roller rolled the chippings flat, to make a smooth surface. The surface was then sprayed with tar.

Improvements in our roads and road surfaces have helped to make today's journeys quicker and more comfortable.

People

Many people help to make journeys possible.

Blacksmiths
Blacksmiths make and fit horseshoes.
A hundred years ago, when most journeys were made in horse-drawn vehicles, this was a very important job. Horses needed new horseshoes every few weeks.

Motoring organisations
In the 1930s, when the advert above appeared, cars were not as reliable as they are today. Motoring organisations, like the AA and RAC, employed people who patrolled the roads on motorbikes, helping any of their members who broke down. Today, they would be called on their mobile phones.

Drivers and conductors

The two men standing beside this bus are the driver and the conductor. The conductor travelled in the bus. He gave the passengers their tickets and let the driver know when to move away from each bus stop. Today, the bus driver usually has to collect the money and give out the tickets, as well as drive the bus.

Across water

Wind power

A hundred years ago, many boats were still powered by the wind.
Ships like the one in the picture on the left were used to carry goods around the coast of Britain and across the sea to other countries.

Engine power

The advert on the right appeared in the early 1930s.
By then, most ships were powered by engines.
Huge passenger ships, called liners, sailed between Britain and America.
Many of the people who travelled on them were emigrating.
This means that they were leaving Britain for ever, to start new lives abroad.

Ferries

Boats were also used to cross short stretches of water. The 1960s picture below shows a car ferry crossing a river. Today, people cross this river by driving through a tunnel.

Many ferries have now been replaced by bridges or tunnels.

People no longer have to queue for the ferry and can cross the water quickly.

Through the air

Powered flight

The first powered flight was made in 1903, in America.
The photograph on the right was taken at a flying display in Britain, in about 1910.
The visitors would have been amazed to see someone flying through the air.

Improvements

During the First World War, which lasted from 1914 to 1918, great improvements were made to planes.
By the 1930s, planes were being used for short passenger flights to cities such as Paris and Brussels.
The planes carried far fewer passengers than they do today.

Faster

By the late 1950s, planes were larger and more reliable.
They could carry more people on longer journeys.
Their engines were more powerful, which made the journeys quicker.

Today, we can fly to the other side of the world in hours.
A hundred years ago, such a journey would have taken weeks by boat.

To work

Every day, people make journeys to and from work.

Walking

A hundred years ago, when this picture was taken, lots of people walked to work.

Many farm workers lived in cottages on the farms where they worked. Their homes were often owned by the person who owned the land.

By bike and bus

In the 1940s, thousands of people worked in factories.
Lots of people travelled to and from work by bike.
Many other people travelled in buses.
The buses in the picture on the right are waiting to take the workers back home at the end of the day.

By car

By the 1950s, lots of people travelled to work by car.
This factory car park shows how popular travelling by car to work had become.
Today, many people still travel to work by car.
Other people choose to travel to work by train, bicycle or motorbike.

On holiday

Charabanc

The people in the 1910s photograph on the right are sitting in a charabanc. Charabancs could be hired to take people on outings to the countryside or the seaside. In those days, few people went on long holidays. Instead, they went on day trips.

Caravan

By the 1950s, more people went on family holidays.
Lots of people enjoyed caravanning. They travelled from one camp site to another, towing the caravan behind their car.
Many people still enjoy caravanning today.

Plane

During the 1970s, when this photograph was taken, foreign holidays became much cheaper than they had been. Many people started to take holidays abroad. They flew on special holiday flights, called charter flights. Spain was a very popular country to visit. Today, people can fly on charter flights to lots of different countries all around the world.

Every day millions of journeys are made by land, sea and air. It is easy to forget that, a hundred years ago, many of the journeys we make today would have been impossible.

Glossary

charabanc an early type of motor coach
chauffeur someone paid to drive another person's car
invention a new object, machine or idea
motoring organisation a business that gives help and advice to car owners
patrolled travelled, keeping a look out
pollution dirt in the air, often from machines
route a particular journey that always follows the same paths or roads
vehicles things that take people or goods from one place to another

Index

Timeline

nearly 120 years ago	nearly 110 years ago	nearly 100 years ago	nearly 90 years ago	nearly 80 years ago	nearly 70 years ago	nearly 60 years ago	nearly 50 years ago	nearly 40 years ago	nearly 30 years ago	nearly 20 years ago	nearly 10 years ago
the 1880s	the 1890s	the 1900s	the 1910s	the 1920s	the 1930s	the 1940s	the 1950s	the 1960s	the 1970s	the 1980s	the 1990s
1880	1890	1900	1910	1920	1930	1940	1950	1960	1970	1980	1990

How to use this book

Each book in this series takes a familiar topic or theme and focuses on one area of the curriculum: science, art and technology, geography or history. The books are intended as starting points, illustrating some of the many different angles from which a topic can be studied. They should act as springboards for further investigation, activity or information seeking.

JOURNEYS

key concepts and activities explored within each book

Science

- journeys involve movement
- all animals can make journeys
- animals can move in different ways
- joints and muscles allow movement
- journeys can be made in vehicles
- many vehicles have engines
- forces make things move
- forces make things speed up and slow down
- forces make things change direction
- energy is needed to make things go

Art and Technology

- roads and vehicles have to be designed
- journeys feature in works of art
- design road signs
- make a wheeled toy vehicle
- investigate flexible ways of joining
- make a toy boat that can move
- test paper gliders
- design an imaginary vehicle
- draw a picture map
- create a 'journey' game

History

changes have taken place during the past one hundred years, relating to:

- the way vehicles are powered
- the uses of vehicles
- the design of vehicles
- the number of car owners
- the design of roads
- the work of people who make journeys possible
- journeys across water and through the air
- journeys to work and journeys on holiday

Geography

- the frequency and distance of journeys can vary
- there are a variety of methods of transport
- there is a difference between public and private transport
- journeys have beginnings and endings
- many people help to make journeys possible
- animals and goods, as well as people, make journeys
- maps are useful when making journeys
- journeys have an impact on the environment